Leopards

by Claire Archer

www.abdopublishing.com

Published by Abdo Kids, a division of ABDO, P.O. Box 398166, Minneapolis, Minnesota 55439.

Copyright © 2015 by Abdo Consulting Group, Inc. International copyrights reserved in all countries. No part of this book may be reproduced in any form without written permission from the publisher.

Printed in the United States of America, North Mankato, Minnesota.

052014

092014

Photo Credits: Glow Images, Shutterstock, Thinkstock

Production Contributors: Teddy Borth, Jennie Forsberg, Grace Hansen

Design Contributors: Candice Keimig, Laura Rask, Dorothy Toth

Library of Congress Control Number: 2013952074

Cataloging-in-Publication Data

Archer, Claire.

 Leopards / Claire Archer.

   p. cm. -- (Big cats)

ISBN 978-1-62970-003-8 (lib. bdg.)

Includes bibliographical references and index.

1. Leopards--Juvenile literature.   I. Title.

599.75--dc23

                    2013952074

Table of Contents

Leopards 4

Hunting 14

Lone Cats 16

Baby Leopards 18

More Facts 22

Glossary 23

Index 24

Abdo Kids Code 24

Leopards

Leopards live in Africa and Asia. They live in many different **habitats**.

4

Leopards prefer **habitats** with many trees. They also like to be near water. They are good climbers and swimmers.

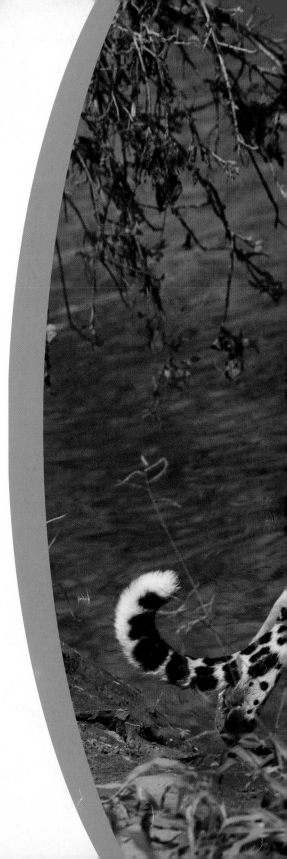

Leopards have light fur.

Their fur has dark spots.

The spots are called **rosettes**.

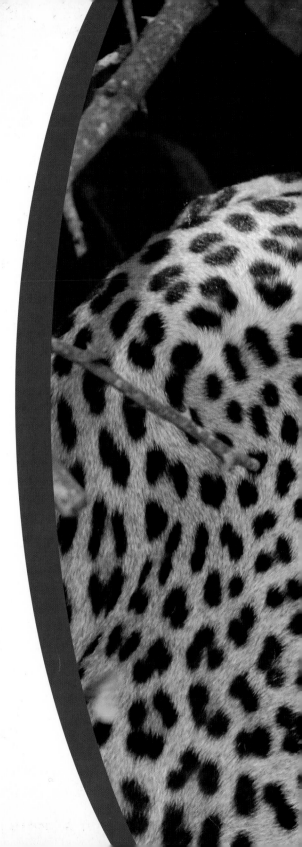

Some leopards are black. Black leopards are sometimes called black panthers.

Leopards rest for most of the day. They often sleep high up in trees.

Hunting

Leopards hunt mainly
at night. They eat fish,
reptiles, and small **mammals**.

14

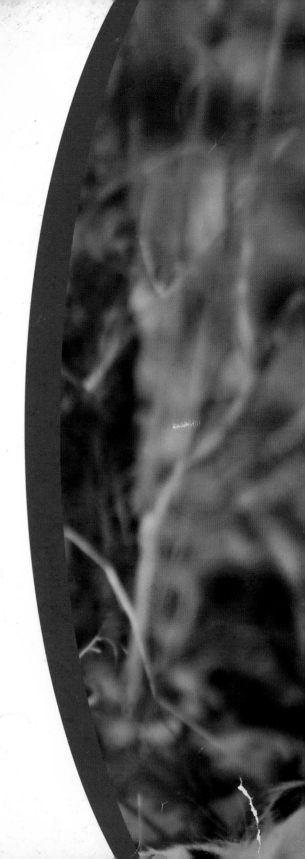

Lone Cats

Leopards spend most of their lives alone. Mothers and babies spend the most time together.

Baby Leopards

Baby leopards are called **cubs**. Their fur is gray when they are born.

Mothers teach their **cubs** how to **survive**. After about two years, cubs are ready to live on their own.

20

More Facts

- Leopards are known to drag their **prey** up into trees. This is to be sure that no other animals eat their meals.

- Leopards have excellent hearing and sense of smell.

- Leopards will purr when they are happy. When they are mad they will growl, roar, and spit.

Glossary

cub – a young animal.

habitat – a place where a living thing is naturally found.

mammal – a member of a group of living things. Mammals make milk to feed their babies and usually have hair or fur on their skin.

prey – an animal hunted or killed by a predator for food.

reptile – a cold-blooded animal with scales. They typically lay eggs on land. Snakes, lizards, and turtles are reptiles.

rosette – a marking that resembles a rose.

survive – to grow and be healthy.

Index

Africa 4

Asia 4

babies 16, 18, 20

behavior 12, 16

black panther 10

fur 8, 10, 18

habitat 4, 6

hunting 14

markings 8

prey 14

abdokids.com

Use this code to log on to abdokids.com and access crafts, games, videos and more!

Abdo Kids Code:
BLK0038